How to Explain CODING to a Grown-Up

RUTH SPIRO

Illustrated by TERESA MARTÍNEZ

ⁱ⌂ⁱ Charlesbridge

When I was a little kid,

I asked a LOT of questions:

How do apples grow?

Where does the sun go at night?

Why do skunks smell bad?

I thought my grown-up had all the answers.

But now that I'm big, I know the truth.
MY GROWN-UP DOES NOT KNOW ALL THE ANSWERS!
Sometimes they need ME to explain things to THEM.
If you're reading this, I'm guessing YOUR grown-up
needs help understanding stuff, too.

With a little help from this book,
YOU can explain CODING to your grown-up!

First, show your grown-up this book.

Whenever your grown-up uses a phone,
they're using a computer.

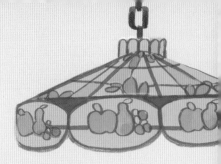

**When dealing with grown-ups, don't
jump into the complicated stuff
too fast. Start with something they
already know.**

Computers are everywhere, and code is what
makes them work.

How exactly can computers do all these amazing things? To start, let's open one up and take a look inside.

Pro Tip

Every now and then it's good to say something surprising, just to make sure your grown-up is paying attention!

Tell your grown-up not to worry.
You do NOT have to open their computer because you have this awesome book.*
It has PICTURES.

*Opening a computer is actually a terrible idea because you could break it.

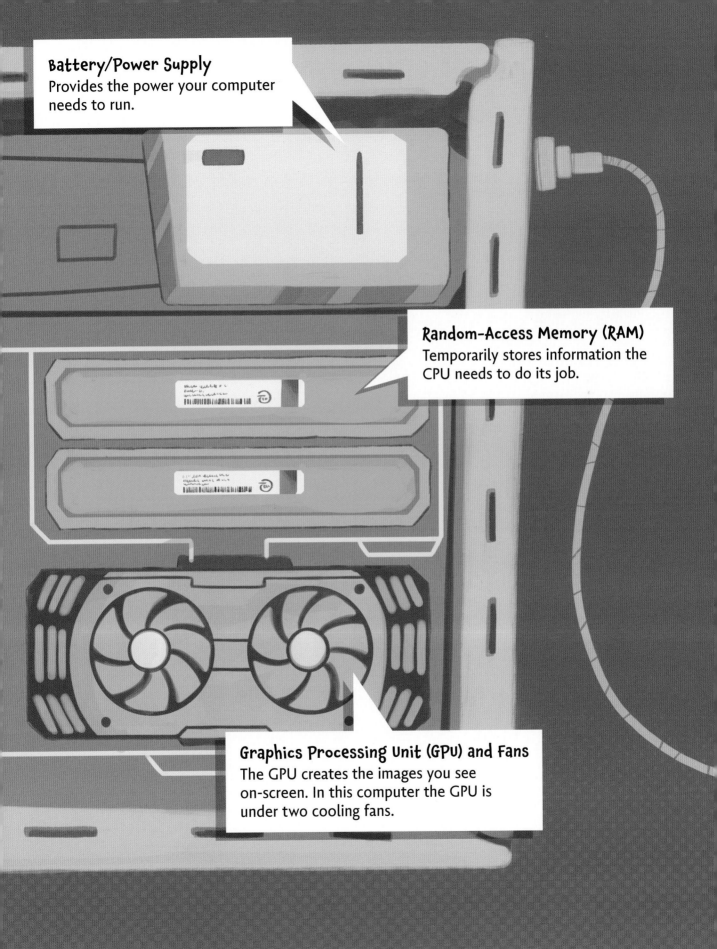

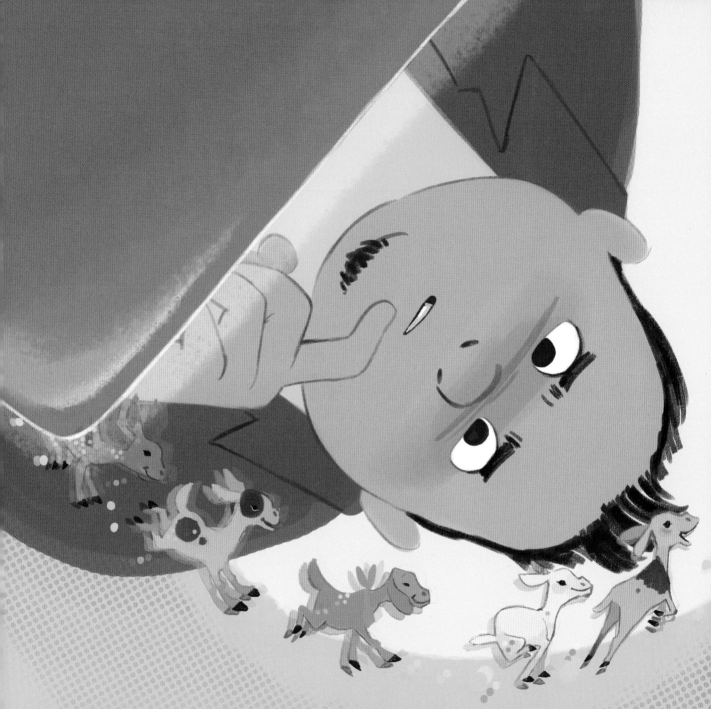

Your grown-up is probably surprised.
And possibly a little confused.

How does all that hardware turn taps on
the keyboard into a video of baby goats
on the screen?

The hardware alone doesn't know what to do.
It needs instructions.

Which brings us to . . .

Coding!

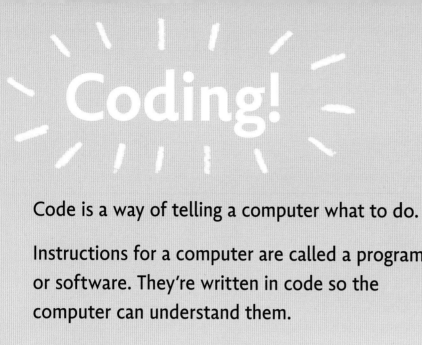

Code is a way of telling a computer what to do.

Instructions for a computer are called a program, or software. They're written in code so the computer can understand them.

Where does code come from?

Someone has to create code.
That person is called a programmer.
They have the super-amazing job of
writing code for computers.
(A lot of people code just for fun, too.)

Pro Tip

Now may be a good time to check in
with your grown-up. Ask if they have
any questions before you move on.

A programmer thinks about what the computer needs to do and figures out the best way to write the instructions. Then they create an algorithm: step-by-step rules in computer code.

Writing a computer algorithm is like walking to the park. You have to take the steps in exactly the right order. Otherwise, you may end up in the wrong place!

Ask your grown-up how they would tell someone to get to the park. Can they write those steps as an algorithm?

Maybe the algorithm looks something like this:

Go out the front door and turn left.

At the bus stop, turn left again.

At the bookstore, look both ways and cross at the light.

Walk one block.

Cross the street.

You're there!

PARK

Some grown-ups don't like to sit still for too long. Invite them to test out their algorithm with a visit to the park!

Pack snacks!

Algorithms tell a computer what to do and can even help it decide what to do next.

Your grown-up may not believe this. If they don't, show them this example:

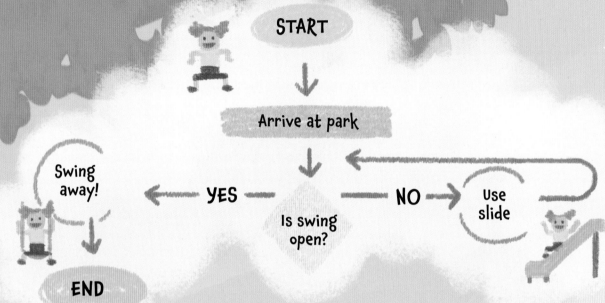

START

Arrive at park

Is swing open?

YES — Swing away! — END

NO → Use slide

This algorithm says to take in data, or information, about whether a swing is open. Then use that data to make a decision:

◆ If a swing is open, then use it.
◆ If a swing is not open, then use the slide instead.

Code that tells a computer how to decide what to do is called a conditional. A conditional says IF something happens, THEN something else happens.

What if you really want a turn on the swing, but someone else is using it?

No problem! We can use the slide for now and then check the swing when we're done. We can repeat these steps again and again until the swing is open.

Data that can change, like whether a swing is open or not, is called a variable. Repeating steps in an algorithm is called a loop.

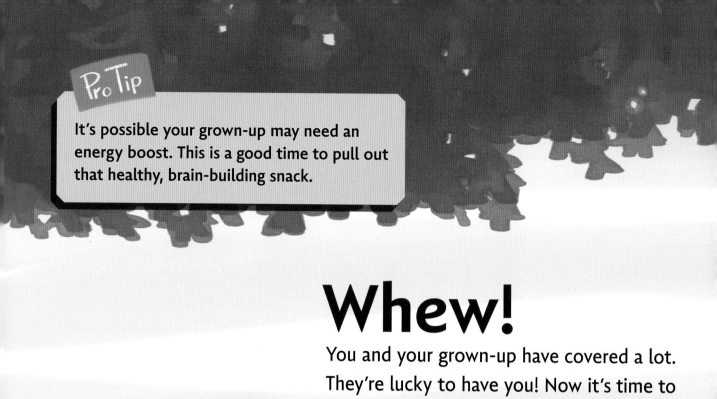

Pro Tip

It's possible your grown-up may need an energy boost. This is a good time to pull out that healthy, brain-building snack.

Whew!

You and your grown-up have covered a lot. They're lucky to have you! Now it's time to pull it all together.

- A software program is a set of instructions that tells a computer what to do.
- It's created by a programmer and written in code so the computer can understand it.
- The computer takes in data and follows the program's instructions.

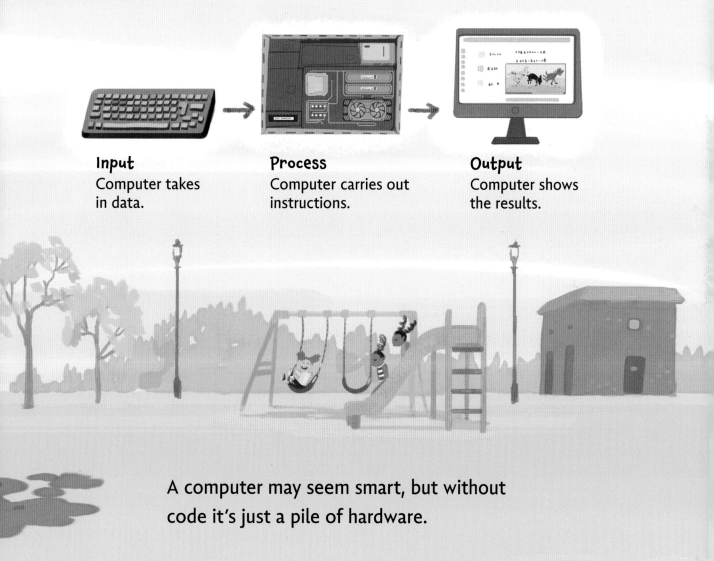

Input
Computer takes in data.

Process
Computer carries out instructions.

Output
Computer shows the results.

A computer may seem smart, but without code it's just a pile of hardware.

Sometimes the computer doesn't do what it's supposed to. It's not the computer's fault. It's just following the program. This usually means there's a mistake in the code.

Programmers call this a bug. They fix the problem by searching through the code to find the bug.

Found it!

Fixing the problem is called debugging.

Pro Tip

Like a programmer, you'll need to approach this step with extreme patience. Some bugs can be very hard to find.

Now that your grown-up knows what code does, they may be interested to see what it looks like. Here's some of the code for deciding whether to use the swing or the slide at the playground:

```cpp
#include "Playground.h"

int main()
{
    bool waiting_for_swing;
    waiting_for_swing = true;

    while (waiting_for_swing)
    {
        if (IsSomeoneOnSwing())
        {
            PlayOnTheSlide();
        }
        else
        {
            PlayOnTheSwing();
            waiting_for_swing = false;
        }
    }

    return 0;
}
```

This is our conditional!

This groups lines of code together.

There's even more code, but it won't all fit on this page!

This is the beginning of the program.

This variable says whether or not we're waiting for the swing.
Yes, we're waiting for the swing.

Anytime we're waiting for the swing, this will happen:

If someone else is on the swing . . .

then we play on the slide.

Otherwise . . .

we play on the swing.
We've had our turn on the swing, so we're not waiting for the swing anymore.

This means everything went great!

Your busy day explaining coding to a grown-up has come to an end. But there's still one thing left to do. Find out what they've learned!

Pro Tip

If your grown-up can explain it, that shows they understand it!

Ask your grown-up, "When we get to a street, how do we know if we should cross? Please answer in coding terms!"

If your grown-up needs a little help, here's a hint!

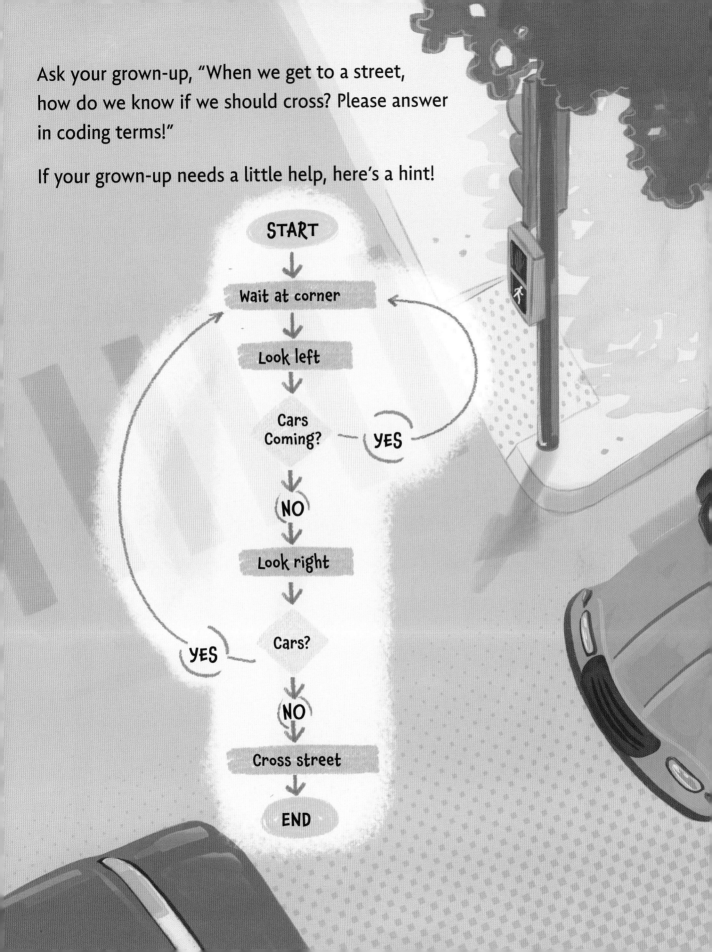

Congratulations!

YOU DID IT!
You explained coding to a grown-up!
Get ready, because now your grown-up
is going to have a LOT more questions.

What will you explain next?

Glossary

algorithm: A set of step-by-step instructions used to complete a task or solve a problem.

bug/debug: A bug is a mistake in a program's code. Debugging is when a programmer looks for the mistake and fixes it.

code: A special system of letters, numbers, and symbols that tells a computer what to do. Programmers write code in different programming languages, such as C++, Java, and Python.

computer: A device that stores and processes data using programs written in code.

conditional: Code written in a format that makes something happen only if something else happens first. A conditional tells a computer how to decide what to do next.

data: Pieces of information that can be stored, organized, and processed by a computer.

hardware: All the parts of a computer you can see or touch, both outside and inside.

loop: Part of a program that repeats itself.

program: The code that tells the computer what to do; also called software.

programmer: A person who plans, writes, and tests the code used by computers. Programmers are good at thinking step by step, solving problems, and working with others on a team.

software: The code that tells the computer what to do; also called a program.

variable: Data that can change based on input.

Computers are everywhere!

How many computers can you and your grown-up find? Look in your home, around your neighborhood, and even up in the sky!

For Alisan, whose enthusiasm for world travel, pizza parties, and
sharing family stories makes her an excellent friend—R. S.

To my brother Pepe—T. M.

Very special thanks to Alisan Miller, software engineer,
for her invaluable expertise and advice.

Text copyright © 2023 by Ruth Spiro
Illustrations copyright © 2023 by Teresa Martínez

Published by Charlesbridge
9 Galen Street, Watertown, MA 02472
(617) 926-0329 • www.charlesbridge.com

Printed in China
(hc) 10 9 8 7 6 5 4 3 2 1

Illustrations created digitally using Photoshop
    and a Wacom tablet
Display type set in Chaloops by The Chank Company
Text type set in Fontanella by Guisela Mendoza
Printed by 1010 Printing International Limited in
    Huizhou, Guangdong, China
Production supervision by Mira Kennedy
Designed by Cathleen Schaad

Library of Congress Cataloging-in-Publication Data
Names: Spiro, Ruth, author. | Martínez, Teresa, 1980–
    illustrator.
Title: How to explain coding to a grown-up / Ruth Spiro;
    illustrated by Teresa Martínez.
Description: Watertown: Charlesbridge, 2023. | Series:
    How to explain science to a grown-up | Audience:
    Ages 4–8 | Summary: "In this tongue-in-cheek guide,
    a kid expert explains to young readers how to teach
    their grown-ups about the basics of coding, including
    hardware, software algorithms, and debugging."
    —Provided by publisher.
Identifiers: LCCN 2022031359 (print) | LCCN 2022031360
    (ebook) | ISBN 9781623543181 (hardcover) |
    ISBN 9781632899743 (ebook)
Subjects: LCSH: Computer programming—Juvenile
    literature.
Classification: LCC QA76.6.S6825 2023 (print) | LCC
    QA76.6 (ebook) | DDC 005.13—dc23/eng/20220716
LC record available at https://lccn.loc.gov/2022031359
LC ebook record available at https://lccn.loc.
    gov/2022031360